FAIRY LORE
AND MYTHS

GREGORY LEE WHITE

White Willow Press
Nashville, TN

Fairy Lore and Myths
by
Gregory Lee White

Text:
Gregory Lee White

Cover Art:
Frank Xavier Leyendecker & Gregory Lee White
Butterfly fairy from the cover of *Life Magazine,* Leyendecker (February 2, 1922)

Proofreading:
Gregory Lee White, Roy Hamilton, Virginia Tabor

Interior Illustrations:
various artists and illustrators from 1880 to the 1930s

First Edition 2023

Published by
White Willow Press
211 Donelson Pike, Suite 111
Nashville, Tn 37214

Printed in the Unites States

ISBN: 978-1-7379306-4-8

TABLE OF CONTENTS

OTHER BOOKS BY GREGORY LEE WHITE

Clucked – The Tale of Pickin Chicken

Making Soap from Scratch: How to Make Handmade Soap – A Beginners Guide and Beyond

Essential Oils and Aromatherapy - How to Use Essential Oils for Beauty, Health, and Spirituality

Little House Search – A Puzzle Book and Tour of the Works of Laura Ingalls Wilder

The Use of Magical Oils in Hoodoo, Prayer, and Spellwork

Papa Gee's Hoodoo Herbal - The Magic of Herbs, Roots, and Minerals in the Hoodoo Tradition

The Stranger in the Cup – How to Read Your Luck and Fate in the Tea Leaves by Gregory Lee White and Catherine Yronwode

How to Use Amulets, Charms, and Talismans in the Hoodoo and Conjure Tradition by Catherine Yronwode and Gregory Lee White

Lenormand Basics – How to Read Lenormand Cards for Beginners

Casting Love Spells – Rituals of Romance, Passion, and Attraction

Hex Appeal – How to Cast Dark Spells of Revenge, Cursing, and Damnation

INTRODUCTION

Fairies are fantastical creatures that are shrouded in fantasy and mystery. They have enchanted us for generations with their charm, magic, and mischief, and they continue to hold the attention of people's imaginations. Even though they are considered mythical, these mysterious beings continue to captivate our interest and entice us to investigate their world and gain a deeper understanding of who they are.

As we travel through fairy lore and legends, we will investigate the various kinds of fairies, where they came from, and the unique characteristics that distinguish them from one another. We will learn about the different types of fairies that exist worldwide, from the teeny-tiny pixies who live in England to the mischievous leprechauns who live in Ireland.

The kingdom of fairies is much more extensive than depicted in children's picture books and bedtime stories. We will take a look at the ways in which fairies have been portrayed in literature, film, and television.

We will explore ways to connect with the fairy realm, including rituals, offerings, and even how to build your own fairy house, dive deeper into plants and herbs that are believed to attract fairies, and learn the significance of each one.

DEDICATION

To everyone who still harbors a childlike faith in the
magic of fairies.

ACKNOWLEDGEMENTS

Many thanks to our friends and business neighbors at
JVI Secret Gardens in Nashville, Tennessee, for installing
our lovely backyard waterfall pond. It was both inspiring
and enchanting to sit beside it while writing this book
about the mystical world of fairies. I would also like to
thank Project Gutenberg, which has provided countless
hours of research by archiving old books that would have
otherwise been lost in time.

MAY THE HALLOWE'EN NUTSHELL
UNTO YOU A GOOD FORTUNE TELL

WHAT IS A FAIRY?

A fairy is a mythological being or legendary creature found in several European nations' folklore, including Celtic, Slavic, Germanic, English, and French folklore. They are a type of spirit that are frequently referred to as metaphysical, supernatural, or preternatural.

Fairy myths and tales synthesize common beliefs from several sources rather than having a single foundation. According to many folk conceptions, fairies originated as either demonized angels or angels in the Christian tradition, deities in Pagan religions, ghosts of the deceased, ancient humans, or spirits of nature.

The term "fairy" has occasionally only been used to describe a certain type of magical being with human-like features, supernatural abilities, and a propensity for deceit. At times, it has been used to refer to any magical being, including gnomes and goblins. The adjective "fairy" has occasionally been employed to denote "enchanted" or "magical," respectively. It also refers to the nation from whence these beings hail, the realm of fairies.

Fairies are typically said to look like humans and possess magical abilities. Over the years, numerous sorts of little fairies have been described, ranging in size from very small to human sized. Instead of being constant, these minuscule sizes might be magically assumed. Some tiny fairies were able to grow into human shapes. On Orkney, fairies were said to be diminutive, clad in dark gray, and occasionally spotted wearing armor. Folklore claims that fairies have green eyes. Fairies are sometimes depicted as having shoes on, and other times as being barefoot. Wings are uncommon in legend; fairies flew by magic and occasionally perched on ragwort stems or the backs of birds; wings are prominent in Victorian and later artwork. Dragonfly or butterfly wings are frequently used in contemporary artwork.

The modern fairy is a mixture of several aspects from traditional belief sources, affected by literature and theory, and does not have a single origin. The mythical aes sdhe, or "people of the fairy hills," have acquired a modern meaning in Irish folklore that includes fairies to some extent. Another source of inspiration were the elves of Scandinavia. Folklorists and mythologists have variably portrayed fairies as the undeserving dead, the offspring of Eve, a type of demon, a species separate from humans, an ancient race of humans, and fallen angels. The mythological or folkloristic elements combine Celtic, Germanic, and Greco-Roman components.

FAIRIES AROUND THE GLOBE

IRELAND

Ireland has a vibrant tradition of folklore, mythology, and narrative, and the world of fairies is one of the most enduring and popular themes in Irish folklore. The Irish have believed for centuries in the existence of a parallel world inhabited by magical creatures that coexist with us but remain hidden from view. These beings are referred to as the "Good People," the "Little People," or simply fairies. They are believed to be both mischievous and benevolent, with the ability to bestow happiness, good fortune, and even prosperity upon those who treat them with reverence.

Irish fairy lore is profoundly rooted in Irish mythology and passed down through generations of storytellers, from pagan beliefs to Christian legends. Irish tradition is rife with intriguing fairy folk from the benevolent 'Sidhe' fairies of the hills to the mischievous leprechauns guarding gold pots at the end of rainbows. Different varieties of fairies are associated with various regions, seasons, and natural elements in Irish fairy tales.

One of the most famous and revered fairy tales in Irish folklore is that of the 'Sidhe' (pronounced 'shee') fairies, also known as the 'Aos Sidhe,' which translates to 'people of the hollow hills.' These fairies are believed to inhabit the ancient mounds and highlands of Ireland and are descended from the Tuatha De Danann, a mythical race of supernatural beings who inhabited Ireland before the Celts arrived. The Sidhe fairies are revered as protectors of the land, animals, and humans who revere and venerate them for their beauty and grace.

The leprechaun, a small faerie renowned for protecting gold pots at the end of rainbows, is another well-known character in Irish fairy tales. Leprechauns are commonly portrayed donning green clothing and top hats and are believed to be shoemakers. They are known for their deceitful nature and are rumored to be able to vanish swiftly if they are pursued.

In Irish mythology, in addition to these more well-known fairy figures, there are numerous other fairy entities, ranging from helpful and friendly to mischievous and malevolent. The Banshee, for instance, is a mythical spirit associated with death and is frequently portrayed as a weeping woman who foretells the death of a family member. The pooka is a malicious fairy creature that frequently assumes the form of a terrifying black horse or other terrifying animals. Even common household items, such as butter and milk, were believed to have their own fairy entities that bestowed good luck or bad luck on those who treated them with respect or disdain.

Despite the advent of modernity, many Irish still believe in fairies. The Irish hold the fae in high regard and continue to inspire art, literature, music, and other forms of creativity.

The role it fostered a sense of community and connectedness among the Irish people is one of the most significant aspects of Irish fairy tales. Fairy folklore allowed the Irish to identify with their history, land, and fellow citizens in a nation that has endured centuries of colonization, oppression, and hardship. Through sharing fairy tales and traditions, the Irish cultivated a sense of shared identity and belonging, which helped sustain them during difficult times.

The Irish fairy folklore is a rich and fascinating tapestry of myth, legend, and tradition that has molded the culture and identity of the Irish for centuries. The world of Irish fairies continues to captivate and enchant people from all over the world, from the benevolent Sidhe fairies who defend the land to the mischievous leprechauns who guard pots of gold and innumerable other fairy creatures in between. Fairies are an integral part of the Irish people's cultural heritage that continues to inspire creativity, community, and a sense of belonging to their land and history.

WALES

In modern Welsh, fairies are called y Tylwyth Teg, which means "the fair people" or "the fair family." This is sometimes made into y Tylwyth Teg yn y

Coed, which means "the fair family in the wood," or Tylwyth Teg y Mwn, which means "the fair people of the mine." They are seen dancing on velvety grass at night under the light of the moon, dressed in blue, green, white, or scarlet robes that are light and flowy. People say that they bless the mortals they choose to bless, and they are also called Bendith y Mamau, or their mother's blessing, which means that they are good children who are a pleasure to know. If you call the fairies a mean name, you make them angry. If you nicely talk about them, you get them to help you. If you study fairy mythology, you can see that this way of talking is a very important fact. People think that the saying "Say only good things about the dead" came from the idea of appeasing the ghost of the dead, who, after leaving his or her body, had gained new powers that could hurt their old friend.

Welsh folklore connects Avalon from the Arthurian legends with the location of fairyland. The triads refer to the green seaside meadows as Gwerddonau Llion. On these islands, a lot of bizarre superstitions still exist. They were said to be the resting place of some Druids' souls who, while not holy enough to reach the Christians' heaven, were also not wicked enough to be sentenced to the tortures of Annwn. So they were given a position in this romanticized version of the purgatorial paradise. The British king Gavran set out with his family into unknown waters in the fifth century to pursue these mythical islands. He was never seen or heard from again. Merlin left in a ship made of glass and never came back. On the Irish Channel, to the west of Pembrokeshire, some seamen still tell tales of the enchanting green meadows that suddenly vanish from view.

GERMANY

In German tradition, various fairies are recorded, but Frau Holle is possibly the best-known. This fairy is reported to reside in a woodland not far from Berchtesgaden and provides the region's winter weather. Frau Holle is said to be able to grant individuals good luck, assist them in locating misplaced belongings, and provide them with cash when they are in need.

The term "moss people" or "moss folk" refers to a category of fairy folk that has been variously linked to dwarfs, elves, or spirits and is depicted in German folklore as having a close relationship with trees and the forest. According to folklore, these fairies might occasionally take things from people or seek assistance, but they would always graciously repay the owners by offering advice or bread. In other myths, the moss people would approach people and ask for human milk to give to their young. Moss people, particularly the females of the species, have the power to unleash plagues while simultaneously having the ability to heal their victims. The Holzfräulein ("Wood women") would emerge from the forest during outbreaks to reveal to the people which medical herbs could treat or prevent plague.

ENGLAND

After the publication of Gervase of Tilbury's Otia Imperialia in the 1400s, fairies gained popularity in England. He was a globetrotter who chronicled his travels in a book. He talked about meeting fairies and other wonderful beings. They had all the same traits: good and wicked, short and tall, ugly and lovely.

But, from what was described in the book, the British conception of fairies changed. The Brits feared fairies because they were perceived as naughty beings capable of casting curses. Instead of pronouncing the word "fairy," which they believed would call them, they said "the Neighbors, the Gentry, or Little People."

Humans used to believe that fairies lived underground, by bodies of water, or far into the woods. They avoided routes rumored to be home to fairies as a result. To avoid obstructing the fairies, some people even went so far as to remove the corners of their homes. They had no intention of thinking about fairy figurines.

As her name suggests, Morgan le Fay, a character from the 1485 book La Morte d'Arthur, is a woman with magical abilities who has a connection to the Faerie realm. Fairies remained a part of the tradition even though they have gradually faded. Although the story of Sir Gawain and the Green Knight is set in the fourteenth century, the Green Knight himself is a supernatural figure. In his novel The Faerie Queene from 1590, Edmund Spenser included fairies. In many literary works, fairies freely coexist alongside the nymphs and satyrs of classical tradition. King Arthur was crowned in "the kingdom of the fairy," according to poet and monk John Lydgate, who also claimed that four fairy queens carried him to Avalon where he is buried beneath a "fairy hill" until he is required once again.

Queen Mary's passionate interest in fairy art and the eight-book series of books by British poet and illustrator Cicely Mary Barker, released from 1923 to 1948, contributed to the widespread popularity of Victorian flower fairies. As time went on, fairies appeared in literature in increasingly pretty and little forms.

Fairies eventually acquired the moniker "Fallen Angels" as a result of the tremendous influence of the era's religion on mythology. The Church supported the idea as a way to exalt God and religion. Christian doctrine claimed that fairies belonged to a kind of "demoted" angels. According to one tale, when a group of angels rebelled, God locked the gates of heaven; those still in heaven continued to be angels; those in hell turned into demons; and those trapped in the middle turned into fairies.

GREECE

In addition to heroes and Olympian deities, ancient Greek stories also feature other legendary beings, such as fairies. Fairies in ancient Greece were known as "nymphs." Nymphs were said to be extremely attractive ladies who were associated to gods like Zeus and Hermes. They were mortals, though. Nymphs frequently resided in sacred trees that the populace revered. These trees had a remarkable, intelligent appearance. A nymph's tree also perished when she did.

Nymphs are the subject of innumerable tales throughout Greek mythology's early centuries. A nymph named Ephydatia fell in love with Hercules' buddy Hylas, hugged him, and dragged him under a lake, causing him to suffocate. As a result, Hylas perished unintentionally. Another well-known nymph is Daphne. She was once pursued by the god Apollon in the woods, but the gods felt sorry for her and changed her into the flower by the same name. Nymphs also spent a lot of time with the satyrs, male nature spirits who frequently pursued them into the forests.

Nymphs came to be referred to as "neraides" and connected with the fairies of Western European folklore as time went on. Neraides are connected to nature. Therefore, during the Middle Ages, people believed they were pagan deities.

Bridal gowns not kept in wardrobes at night are said to be vulnerable to neraide theft in several Greek communities. Young males who are alone in nature and wonder can also be "stolen" by neraides. They will play the field and guide them into various spheres. If the do men come back, they are different, no longer the same person they once were.

JAPAN

The Japanese word "yosei" is frequently used interchangeably with the English word "fairy." This term is most often used to describe spirits from Western myths, but it can also infrequently apply to a figure from Japanese folklore. For instance, old folktales claim that people formerly feared the y'sei could bring the dead back to life. It is also mentioned that the inhabitants of Mount Hrai are tiny fairies, unaware of enormous harm, and as a result, their hearts never age. In their folklore, the Ainu also mention a small race of humans known as the Koro-pok-guru. The Kijimuna, tree sprites described in the Ryukyuan religion of Okinawa, are another fairy-like entity from Japan.

from the storybook, *A Round Robin*, by M. A. Hoyer and Robert Ellice
Mack, illustrated by Harriett M. Bennett, circa 1891.

FAIRIES IN LITERATURE, MOVIES, AND TELEVISION

A MIDSUMMER NIGHT'S DREAM

In Shakespeare's play, we are introduced to several fairies, the fairy queen Tatiana and the mischievous character Puck, and the four fairy attendants to the queen: Peaseblossom, Cobweb, Moth, and Mustardseed. Shakespearean fairies are said to be relatively tiny. Ariel from The Tempest and the fairies from A Midsummer Night's Dream are compared to cowslips, a flower. This is significant since fairies were frequently imagined to be on par with humans in terms of size in the folklore of the time. These characters, however, would have been portrayed by average-sized human actors when the play was staged.

MALEFICENT

Not every fairy is friendly. The story of Sleeping Beauty is evidence that some of them are out to curse you. Disney created Maleficent, whereas the story of Sleeping Beauty traces back many centuries. Maleficent, Sleeping Beauty's live-action reimagining, rehabilitated her 55 years after her first appearance as a villain in the animated film Sleeping Beauty in 1959. A special mention must also be made of the good fairies in this narrative. In some versions, a dozen good fairies guard Sleeping Beauty, but only three are in the Disney version: In the live-action remake and its sequel, Flora, Fauna, and Merryweather are referred to as Knotgrass, Thistlewit, and Flittle. Of course, in the Angelina Jolie movie, we find that Maleficent has been greatly wronged, which has turned her bitter; she is, in fact, not evil.

THE SUGAR PLUM FAIRY

Keira Knightley's portrayal of the Sugar Plum Fairy in The Nutcracker and the Four Realms (2018) is one of the most contemporary versions of the character. This fairy, who rules over the realm of treats, can be traced back to The Nutcracker. Although neither the original storybook nor its subsequent adaptation mentions her by name, Tchaikovsky's ballet brought her to life.

TINKER BELL

She is possibly the most well-known faerie. She has an entire line of her own films. When he wrote Peter Pan, the Scottish playwright J.M. Barrie created Tinker Bell. Since then, she has appeared on stage (typically represented by a light and some chimes) and on screen, most notably in the 1953 Disney animation and in Hook, where Julia Roberts portrayed her.

SOOKIE STACKHOUSE

Sookie Stackhouse is a fictional character and the protagonist of Charlaine Harris' book series, The Southern Vampire Mysteries, on which the popular

HBO series True Blood is based. Sookie is a telepathic hybrid of humans and faeries known as a halfling. In the universe of True Blood, consuming fairy blood will grant vampires the ability to walk in the sunlight, resulting in the near extinction of the fae. Sookie encounters Queen Mab during a brief visit to the realm of the fairies. Queen Mab is a faerie mentioned in William Shakespeare's play Romeo and Juliet, where she is referred to as "the midwife of the fairies." Later, she appears in additional poetry and literature, as well as in a variety of roles in drama and film.

THE FAIRY GODMOTHER

Without her Fairy Godmother, Cinderella would be in quite a pickle. Without a doubt, she would still be expected to clean up after her stepmother and stepsisters. Cinderella's Fairy Godmother grants her wish to attend the royal ball in style by providing her with a magnificent gown and carriage, which morphs into a pumpkin on the way home. While the Fairy Godmother isn't the focus of Cinderella, she plays a significant role in the story.

THE TOOTH FAIRY

We must include an honorable mention - the tooth fairy. While mainly found in folklore, the tooth fairy, or sometimes just the mention of her, can be found in numerous television programs and movies going back decades. According to the legend surrounding the tooth fairy, if a child loses one of their baby teeth, they should lay it under their pillow or on their nightstand, and the Tooth Fairy will come by while they are sleeping to replace the missing tooth with a small gift. Parents frequently see the myth as offering solace to kids who have lost a tooth. According to research, a youngster who is afraid or in agony due to losing a tooth may find consolation in believing in the Tooth Fairy.

A custom known as "tand-fé," or tooth fee, was practiced in Northern Europe and was paid when a child lost their first teeth. The Eddas, the first documented account of Norse and Northern European customs, was composed around 1200, and they describe this tradition. Children's teeth and other items belonging to children were believed to bring good luck in combat in Norse culture, and Scandinavian warriors wore a necklace of children's teeth around their necks.

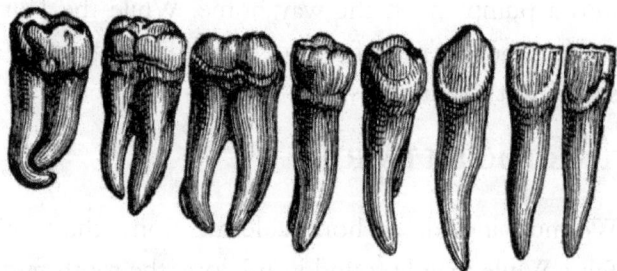

TYPES OF FAIRIES

Some say there are numerous types of fairies. Fairies, especially those found in Irish, English, Scotch, and Welsh tradition, have undergone several classifications. These definitions often concentrate on behavior or physical qualities and may not necessarily correctly reflect local traditions. I have tried to provide a fairly extensive list of the types of fairies you might encounter but, be aware, there are many more.

Asrai - a water sprite that has characteristics like mermaids. She is stunningly gorgeous, yet she only shows her face once every century. It is claimed that Asrai lives in the depths of the ocean and can only be grown in the glow of the moon. Asrai has a morbid aversion to sunlight, and she will perish instantly if exposed to it.

Banshee - a well-known Irish fairy whose mournful wails are considered omens of death. A banshee is a female fairy who wails to warn a family of the impending death of a member of the household. She can appear as a beautiful woman or a hag in untidy garments. Banshee is commonly referred to as the Death Messenger due to the widespread belief that she can predict when someone would die.

Brownie - a kind of fairy known for its selfless service to the elderly and the sick. Brownies are sometimes mistaken for hobgoblins due to their dark skin and hair, hence the name. Brownies are invisible to the naked eye but not to those with the ability of second sight. Brownies can shape-shift, allowing them to take on a variety of appearances. Most of the time, they like to assume the appearance of farm animals. Brownies will do chores around the house for food and honey.

Devas - a type of little fairy that resembles a firefly. You have probably seen devas without realizing it if you live in a wooded environment. Devas can be seen all across the natural world, but the forests are where you're most likely to encounter one. It was in Persia and Greece that the deva first appeared. Those unwell and wanting to use plants as medicine often turn to the Devas for assistance.

Dryad - these creatures are bound to trees and are a subset of fairies. A dryad is a type of fae who lives in trees and suffers the same fate as the tree if it is cut down. Dryads rarely venture out of the safety of the trees they call home. They have a strong sense of place and will do anything to protect the survival of their beloved tree. If humans take good care of their trees, these fae will view them more favorably.

Elf - forests, caves, hills or rocks, and springs are where some believe elves make their homes. They have keen hearing and eyesight and are naturally graceful and agile. Pointed ears, big, expressive eyes, and other attractive facial traits are typical of elves.

Although elves do not possess immortality, they do enjoy exceptional lifespans. It's common knowledge that elves have an innate resistance to evil forces.

Gnomes - the legend of Gnomes has its roots in Scotland, but the folk belief that they can be found in any forest is widespread. Gnomes thrive in verdant environments because they are so in one with nature. Gnomes resemble dwarfs in appearance. Rapid maturation contributes to their old-looking appearance.

Kobolds - a species of fairy that is exclusively found in mines and interacts with miners. While some Kobolds are troublemakers who destroy the miners' work, others will help or bang on the tunnels to warn them of an impending cave-in.

Leprechauns - said to reside in Ireland and are typically seen wearing bright green and red. Leprechauns are sneaky little fairies who make their living making shoes in isolation. Humans are granted three wishes when they capture leprechauns in exchange for their freedom.

Pixies - small fairies that have large heads, pointy noses and ears, and gossamer wings. They are kind fairies but are known for playing tricks on unsuspecting travelers. They are flower lovers and often help out around the house. Pixies can transform into numerous beings or forms by using their shape-shifting abilities. Pixies can also grow or shrink in size.

1900 Ad Murray & Lanmans Florida Water Fairy Flowers

FAIRY RINGS

The mythology around fairy rings is extensive. They go by the titles ronds de sorcières ("witches' circles") in French and Hexenringe ("witches' rings") in German, which alludes to their magical origins. According to German folklore, fairy rings indicate the location where witches danced on Walpurgis Night, and according to Dutch belief, the rings indicate the location of the Devil's milk churn. In Tyrol, it was believed that flying dragons' fiery tails created fairy rings, and that for seven years only toadstools could grow there. European folklore frequently forbade anyone from entering a fairy ring. According to French folklore, enormous toads with bug eyes guarded the fairy rings and would curse anyone who ventured outside of them. If you entered a fairy ring in another region of Europe, you would lose one eye. The use of fairy rings in the Philippines connects fairies and small spirits.

Fairy rings, according to Western European traditions including English, Scandinavian, and Celtic, are the consequence of elves or fairies dancing. The Middle English name elferingewort ("elf-ring"), which means "a ring of daisies caused by elves' dancing," dates to the 12th century, indicating that such concepts have existed at least since the medieval era.

Due in part to the same belief that they both dance in circles, Victorian folklorists connected fairies and witches. Since the rings are only visible to mortals the next morning, these celebrations are mainly linked with moonlit evenings. Superstition considers fairy circles sacrosanct and forbids anybody from entering them lest they enrage the fairies and curse them (for example, a farmer entering with a plow).

There are many stories about what happens when humans enter a fairy ring. People believe they will die young if they step into an empty fairy ring. A Somerset tradition from the 20th century says that a murderer or thief who walks into the fairy ring will be hanged. Most of the time, if someone breaks a fairy boundary, they become invisible to people outside the circle and may be unable to leave. Often, the fairies make people dance until they are too tired, die, or go crazy. In Welsh stories, fairies try to get people to join them in their dancing circles.

Etched book illustration, Fairy Ring, 1873

HOW TO WORK WITH FAIRIES

Working with fairies can add a sense of supernatural wonder to your practice and make a place feel like a home. Just remember that not all faeries are good and generous; there is frequently a cunning, trickster element among them. The more you learn about them and the various kinds of beings there, the easier it will be for you to interact with them. The energy they provide your magic will be a remarkable reward if they become friends with you.

The first thing you want to do is clean and cleanse your space. By cleaning, I mean tidying things up:

- Plant flowers.

- Keep the yard trimmed.

- Remove any debris.

- Replace or remove any plants that have died.

Cleansing is a spiritual act where you might burn incense or sage to clear away any negative energy. This includes keeping negative people out of your space. When you are in the area where you want to attract the Fae, keep your thoughts clean and avoid negative or bad language. You might even write your own ritual where you play soft music, sit in the nature of your yard, and invite them to come in. If fairies do enter your space, treat them with respect when asking for help or having anything done for you. Ask nicely, always leave an offering, and express your gratitude. They are not fond of demands, and doing so can backfire on you.

Many people like to put out little fairy houses for them. Natural materials like wood, bark, stones, etc. should be used to construct fairy homes. Fairies are natural beings, so they are not particularly drawn to plastic. Create a base for your fairy house out of a piece of cardboard or scrap wood and decorate it with stones, moss, or grass. Then, using wood glue to hold them together, stack twigs, crisscrossing them with each layer to create logs for the house's walls. Also, you need to make a hole for the door. Not only is moss useful as bedding, but it also makes a fantastic, waterproof roof for your home. To build a walkway going up to the door, collect flat stones.

CRYSTALS AND STONES

In addition to their glitter, fairies also adore crystals and gemstones for their ties to the soil. Every member of the quartz family will boost your garden's energy and add some bling, but some types can be especially beneficial. If you use little lights in your garden, the clear quartz, which is highly reflective, will absorb the color and amplify the brightness.

The numerous colors of aura quartz are all incredibly luminous. Nevertheless, titanium quartz, commonly called rainbow aura quartz, is the most vibrantly colored and uplifts the spirit.

Peridot can be used to speak with all kinds of nature spirits, including those from the plant and animal worlds and the fairy realms. It is an excellent stone for earth and animal healers. Geodes can be placed outside to draw faeries who live in caves.

Hagstones or Fairy Stones are any stone with a hole running straight through it that, just by being in your hands, possesses magical, spiritual, or religious properties. These peculiar holes result from erosion from water moving or flowing past the stones and through them. Stones colliding with one another along a sca or riverbed produce the stones.

Rose quartz encourages unconditional love and may draw sweet fairies. Amethyst increases our sensitivity to the intangible energies around us and can make us more aware of the presence of fairies. Linked to the sun, citrine is thought to ward off evil fairies.

OFFERINGS

So, you have cleaned up the area, cleaned up your act, burned your incense, and laid out some shiny gemstones. Next, you want to give the fairies offerings.

Fairies love foods that are sweet or rich. Some of the most popular foods to offer them are milk or cream, butter, honey, unwrapped candy, small cakes, ale or alcohol, fresh fruit, and good bread. It is said they love foods sprinkled with saffron and that nettle tea is their favorite drink - a good reason to plant nettle in the garden.

Other offerings include coins, bells, shells, jewelry, silver, or gold.

FLOWERS TO USE IN A FAIRY GARDEN

Huge flowering plants conjure up images of fairies bathing in the dew or using them as parasols. Even the vegetation plays a part in the fairy garden by casting shadows and providing hiding places for timid fairies. Every plant that draws hummingbirds, butterflies, and bees will also draw fairies. Children adore spending time with these wild animals and admiring the flowers' vibrant colors.

Bee Balm - denotes good health and defense against illness and evil.

Columbine - for bravery, to ward off envy, in charms to draw genuine love and get lost love back, and to attract fairies

Cosmos - cosmos flowers are used to create harmony and order since they stand for, peace, love, modesty, and balance.

Foxglove - foxglove juice or dew can be used in ritual to communicate with faeries, and the leaves are thought to be capable of removing faerie enchantments.

Heather - is perfect for safety, good fortune, and eternal life. Carry with you to shield you against crime or abuse.

Honeysuckle - used to bind a love interest to you. When infused in an oil, can be used to anoint the forehead to increase psychic vision.

Mallow - carrying mallow will bring you affection. The flowers are used in altar decoration, garlands, and Beltane rituals.

Roses - besides love, roses are linked to female intuition, dream work, avoiding conflict, beauty, confidence, truth, and passion.

Nasturtium - for emotional wellness, to promote compassion, and for victory over struggles.

Pansies - use in all your romantic spells; they can both deepen and improve existing relationships and draw in fresh ones. Use in spells that bring rain.

Petunia - gives you protection, hope, balance, and the chance to reach your full potential.

Primrose - the primrose flower is often associated with the month of February. It stands for patience, kindness, and gentleness.

Snapdragon - strengthens any protection ritual and

can stop people from lying to you.

Sunflower - used in religious ceremonies by the Aztecs to honor the gods of the sun. Sunflowers can bring fertility, happiness, luck, healing, and loyalty.

Tulip - symbolizes hope, perfect love, and making a fresh start

Violet - a sign of modesty, shyness, and humility. Can be used for protection spells and to make people more faithful.

HERBS AND FRUITS FOR THE FAIRY GARDEN

Fairies are drawn to the blossoms on fruit-bearing trees, and the fruit itself serves as a food source for them. Herbs are believed to entice them to the garden, especially when they are in abundance.

Apples - the fruit and tree are connected to wealth, love, creativity, longevity, and fertility. Because apples have a five-pointed star in the middle, they are often linked to witchcraft.

Clover - for prosperity, success, love, fidelity, and money. Blesses and guards domesticated animals.

Elderberries - A shield against dark spells and a strong defense against evil spirits.

Mint - used for healing and purification, peppermint

has also been used as a rub or wash on doors and furniture to expel negativity and evil. Protects the home against illness. Spread peppermint around the altar for help in performing magic.

Mugwort - for psychic ability, astral travel, and used to clean stones and amulets when brewed as a tea.

Mushrooms - Victorian fairy lore linked toadstools, mushrooms, and hollow hills with elves, pixies, and the unintentional transportation of individuals to fairyland, a world of shifting perspectives teeming with elemental spirits. There is a belief that mushrooms are the gateway between our world and the land of fairies. Thus, they are associated with good luck, spiritual enlightenment, and mystical power.

Nettle - powerful protector, used nettle to break a jinx and send it back to the one who cast it. Worn as a talisman to keep negativity away. Used in purification baths.

Plums - love, spirituality, leisure, passion, longevity, knowledge, and rebirth.

Rosemary - often used in spells of fidelity and to end jealousy. Used often for ritual cleansing by steeping rosemary in the bath water. Protection, purification.

St. John's wort - worn as an amulet, it is believed to offer protection from cuts caused by swords, knives, and bullets, and when hung above barn and stable doors at midsummer, it shields the cattle from the bad deeds of witches and demons.

Thyme - keeping nightmares away, purification, love, abundance, and courage.

Wood sorrel - compassion, joy, spiritual healing, and maternal care. Associated to woodland spirits, elves, and fairies.

Yarrow - used for healing, courage, self-esteem, and for overcoming fear. Taking a ritual bath with yarrow is said to increase psychic abilities. Also used to break curses.

Another fairy inspired Murray & Lanman Florida Water
advertisement. Circa 1900

THE FAIRY STORIES

When I research a book, I often turn to books that are out of print, looking for jewels of information that aren't found in the mainstream. Some of these works are over a century old. Old books are a significant part of our cultural heritage. They reflect the thoughts, ideas, and beliefs of a particular time period and can offer a unique glimpse into history.

So, when I began researching the fairy people, I came across two interesting titles. The first was Ancient Legends, Mystic Charms, and Superstitions of Ireland by Lady Wilde. First published in 1887, I had the pleasure of reading the 1919 reprint edition. The folklore author Lady Francesca Wilde was well-known. In the book, she covers many stories of Ireland, with over 300 pages on fairies, superstitions, herbal remedies, witches, art, music, rituals and spells, and the everyday folklore of the Irish people. She researched several Irish folktales, speaking directly to those who had first heard the tales to get the specifics.

The second book I turned to was British Goblins: Welsh Folklore, Fairy Mythology, Legends, and Traditions by the author Wirt Sikes, published in 1888. Sikes's book is over 350 pages of folklore revolving around the Welsh countryside, where he talks about everything from fairies to ghosts, mythology, King Arthur, and praying at the crossroads.

I have taken fifteen stories from these books and rewritten them in our modern-day language while, hopefully, maintaining some of their old-world charm. You may find thoughts and ideas that we no longer subscribe to in the 21st century, but by the same token, you may unearth jewels of information that have been long forgotten. The thought of losing hundreds of stories and folklore tales, because a book has long been out of print is sad to me. I am grateful that there are places like Project Gutenberg (www.gutenberg.org) that are working to keep these books and information archived for people to learn from and enjoy. If you find the stories I've chosen interesting, I encourage you to go to their website and read the books in their entirety.

THE FAIRY RATH

The ancient rath, fort, or liss generally enclosed about a half-acre and had two or more defensive fortifications constructed by the tribal leaders. When the race of chieftains died out, however, the Sidhe flocked to the forts, where they held their councils, celebrations, and dances; and if a man placed his ear close to the ground at night, he could hear the sweet music of the fairies rising from beneath the earth.

The rath forever after is sacred to the fae, and no mortal is permitted to cut down a tree or remove a stone from it. However, building on a faerie rath would be especially risky. No human hand should venture to touch the ancient dancing grounds of the fairies.

People claim that it is improper to sing or whistle "The pretty girl milking her cow" at night because it is a fairy melody, and fairies will not tolerate a mortal singing their music while they are dancing on the grass. If a person sleeps on the rath, however, the music will penetrate his soul, and when he awakens, he may sing the melody he heard in his dreams.

This is how the bards learned their songs, and they became such accomplished musicians and harpists that the fairies, though invisible to mortal eyes, frequently gathered to listen.

REVENGE OF THE FAIRIES

The fairies strongly protest to the fairy raths, where they gather at night, being developed. With plenty of money, a farmer named Johnstone purchased some land and picked the site the fairies favored the most to construct a home on since it was a lovely, lush area.

He was told by the neighbors that it was a fairy rath, but because he was from the north, he laughed and didn't care and dismissed their warning as nothing more than old wives' stories. As no one else in the neighborhood was as wealthy as the Johnstones after he built the house and made it a pleasure to live in, the locals assumed the farmer had discovered a pot of gold in the fairy rath.

But, the fairies were always thinking of ways to punish the farmer for taking away their dancing area and for destroying the hawthorn bush where they conducted their moonlit celebrations. A small, elderly woman wearing a blue cloak approached Mrs. Johnstone one day as the cows were being milked and requested a porringer of milk.

There won't be any tramps visiting my home. You won't get any milk from me, the lady of the house commanded. She also instructed the agricultural workers to drive her away.

The best and finest cow eventually fell ill, stopped

producing milk, lost her horns and teeth, and passed away.

The same little girl in the blue cloak then appeared in front of Mrs. Johnstone while she was seated in the parlor spinning flax.

She requested some fresh cakes off the griddle to take with her. "Your maids are baking cakes in the kitchen," she remarked.

The farmer's wife growled, "Get out of here; you are a cruel old creature, and you poisoned my best cow." And she instructed the farm workers to use sticks to drive her away.

The Johnstones only had one child at this point, a handsome, intelligent lad who was full of life and merriment and as powerful as a young colt. He claimed that the fairies gathered around him at night and beat and squeezed him while others sat on his chest, preventing him from breathing or moving. Shortly after this, he started to act unusual and strangely, and he started to have trouble sleeping. And they threatened never to let him be alone unless he pledged to feed them a griddle cake and a porringer of milk for supper every night. In order to calm the youngster, the mother placed these items on a table next to his bed every night. The next morning, they were gone.

But, the boy continued to cry out, and his eyes took on a peculiar, crazy appearance, as if he had no idea of anything nearby or in his immediate surroundings but felt concerned by something that was far, far away. When they questioned him about his condition, he replied that every night, fairies took him away to the hills, where he would dance with them until daylight, at which point they would bring him back and lay him in his bed once more.

The farmer and his wife finally reached their breaking point from anguish and despair as they watched the infant wailing helplessly in front of them with nothing they could do to comfort him. He cried out in excruciating pain one night—

"Mom! mother!" His eyes were wild with fear. "The fairies are killing me; they are here on my chest, pressing me to death, so send for the priest to remove them."

The farmer and his wife did not believe in fairies or priests, but they complied with the child's request and summoned the priest, who prayed for him and doused him in holy water in order to calm him.

While the priest prayed, the sad little man appeared to become calmer. He claimed the fairies were leaving him and left him alone before falling asleep peacefully. Yet, when he awoke the next morning, he reported to his parents that he had a magnificent dream of strolling through a beautiful garden with angels. He recognized this to be heaven, and he predicted that he would arrive there before nightfall because the angels had promised to come for him.

They then kept an eye on the sick youngster throughout the night because they could see that he still had a fever, but they hoped that something would change before dawn because he was now sleeping well and grinning.

He awoke and sat up as the clock struck midnight, and when his mother embraced him while sobbing, he said, "The angels are here, Mother," before he dropped back and passed away.

After this catastrophe, the farmer never raised his head again. He stopped taking care of his farm, the animals died, the crops failed, and before a year and a day had passed, he was buried next to his young son. The land then changed hands, and the home was demolished because no one wanted to live in it. The fairies once again danced there in the moonlight as they did in the past, unhindered and joyful, and the bad spell was broken for good. No one, however, would plant on the rath, so the grass grew again all over it, green and lovely.

A warning to anyone who would provoke the vengeance of the fairies by interfering with their historical rights, belongings, and privileges, the childless mother fled back to her own people after the people refused to interact with them.

FAIRY DANCE

The following is an Irish folktale told by a local of the Western Islands, where old beliefs are held with all the vigor of youth.

The most beautiful girl on the island was killed when she stumbled on the way to get water one night in late November, the month when spirits have the most influence. It was a portent of bad luck, and when she stood up to survey her surroundings, she had the distinct impression that she had been transported to an unfamiliar place where everything had been altered, as if by magic. From afar, she spotted a large group of people congregating around a roaring fire, and she was gradually attracted closer to them until she found herself in the middle of the crowd. The people were silent, staring intently at her, and she was terrified. Then, a handsome young man dressed like a royal, in a red31 sash and a golden band in his long yellow hair, approached her and requested if he could invite her to dance.

She responded, "That is a silly thing of you, sir, to ask me to dance," when there was, in fact no music to dance to.

Then he raised his hand and signaled the crowd, and immediately the sweetest music began to play near her and all around her, and the young man took her hand and they danced and danced until the moon and the stars went down, but she seemed to float above it all, and she forgot about everything except the dancing, and the sweet low music, and her beautiful partner.

The music stopped, and after a heartfelt thank you, her dance partner encouraged her to join the group for dinner. The young man who had seemed to be their monarch led her down a set of steps she had previously not noticed, and the rest of the group soon followed. A large hall adorned with gold, silver, and lights awaited them at the top of the stairs, and within it, they found an abundance of delicious food and wine served in golden goblets. When she sat down, everyone urged her to eat and drink, and since she was tired from dancing, she accepted the prince's golden cup and brought it to her lips. At that very moment, a man brushed up to her and murmured,

"If you eat or drink anything, you will never get back home."

She put down the cup and said that she would not be drinking. This infuriated them, and a commotion erupted, at which point a tall, dark-skinned man spoke up in a menacing tone:

"If you drink with us, you're one of us."

He grabbed her arm and put the wine to her lips, scaring the life out of her. At that very moment, though, a man with fiery hair stepped forward and took her by the hand, leading her away.

"You are safe for the time being," he reassured me. No one can hurt you as long as you carry this herb in your hand all the way home. And he presented her with a cutting from the Athair-Luss (the ground ivy). 4

She grabbed this and ran as fast as she could along the grassy field, but she could hear footsteps following close behind. Finally, she made it home, locked the door behind her, and went to bed. Suddenly, a commotion broke out outside, and she heard voices calling out to her.

With the enchantment of the herb, we have lost control over you, but when you dance to the music on the hill once more, you will remain with us forever, and no one can stop you.

But she guarded the magic branch, and the fairies stopped bothering her; however, she danced to the song of the fairies that November night on the hillside with her fairy lover, and the music remained in her ears for a very long time.

RACE OF THE FAIRIES

The Sidhe, or spirit race, are also known as the Feadh-Ree, or fairies, and legend has it that they were originally angels who were cast out of heaven for their arrogance.

Long before humans were made, some of these beings crashed to Earth and made their homes here. They come up on the land on moonlit nights, riding their white horses, to celebrate with their fairy kin of the earth, who dwell in the clefts of the hills, to dance together on the greensward under the ancient trees, and to drink nectar from the cups of the flowers, which is the fairy wine. Other fairies fell into the sea and built beautiful fairy palaces of crystal and pearl beneath the waves.

However, other fairies are demonic and prone to evil and malice because they were expelled from heaven and now reside in hell, where the devil rules them and sends them on terrible missions to lure men's souls down into the depths of sin and pleasure. The devil chooses a select few evil humans and bestows upon them the ability to conjure incantations, brew love potions, cast wicked spells, and take on a variety of shapes through the use of magical plants. These spirits dwell beneath the earth and teach only the evilest humans their secrets.

The women who have been taught by them and have

thus become instruments of the Evil One are the terror of the neighborhood, for they have all the power of the fairies and all the malice of the devil, who reveals to them the secrets of times and days, the secrets of herbs, and the secrets of evil spells, and by the power of magic, they can effect all their purposes, whether good or evil.

The fairies of this world are tiny yet fascinating creatures. They have an insatiable appetite for song and dance, enjoy lavish lifestyles in palaces tucked away in the hills and hidden caverns high in the mountains, and stock their enchanted abodes with all kinds of beautiful furnishings thanks to the immense influence of their magic. Yet they frequently succumb to the allure of a mortal woman's beauty and the strong desire to have her as a wife. Until the end of time, when they are destined to disappear forever, they can take on any appearance they want and are immune to death. But they look down on humanity because of our promise of eternal life and our superior stature.

Beautiful eyes and a daring, carefree nature have always marked them as members of the Sidhe, or spirit race. The offspring of such unions tend to inherit a weird mystic temperament and achieve great success in the arts, especially the performing arts. Nonetheless, they are hostile, angry, and difficult to live with.

The fairy king and princes wear green outfits, with red crowns that are topped with golden fillets. The fairy queen and her great court ladies dance on the greensward, their long golden hair sweeping the ground as they wear shimmering silver gauze robes encrusted with 39 diamonds.

Hawthorn trees are revered to the fairies and often serve as the focal point of fairy rings; a local farmer would rather die than tear down one of these ancient trees. Yet, no one ever worships faeries because the Sidhe are considered subhuman. They also have a healthy respect for the mystical fairy power but are terrified of it, thus, they never intentionally provoke it.

The Sidhe are always on the lookout for good-looking kids to kidnap and raise in their stunning subterranean fairy palaces before marrying them off to other fairies when they reach adulthood.

The villagers are terrified that a fairy changeling may be left in the cradle instead of their own beautiful child. If a wrinkly infant is discovered in the cradle, they may remove it at night and bury it in an open grave in the hopes that their child will be returned to them in the morning.

It is stated that once every seven years, the fairies

kidnap a human child to sacrifice to the devil in exchange for the power he grants them. And lovely girls of all ages are abducted for sacrifice or marriage to the fairy king.

In keeping with their pristine demeanor, fairies appreciate having access to a pail of clean water each night.

Because they are so morally upright, they also take pleasure in fine wines and always make sure to bless those who help them. In ancient times, the great lords of Ireland routinely put a keg of the finest Spanish wine on the window sill overnight for the fairies, only to find that it had vanished by morning.

Fire is the most sacred of all created things, and only man has control over it, making it an excellent safeguard against fairy magic. To this day, no animal has figured out how to coax fire's spirit out of its resting place in stone or wood. A ring of fire around livestock or a child's cradle, or fire beneath the churn, will prevent damage from the fairies. All fairy magic, if any, is doomed to be extinguished by the fire spirit.

FAIRY HELP - THE PHOUKA

If the farmer is kind to the Phouka, the Phouka will return the favor by helping him with his labor. Something swept past the farmer's kid like the wind one day as he watched over the cattle in the field, but the boy was unfazed since he knew it was the Phouka on his way to the old mill by the moat, where the fairies congregated each night. Finally, he yelled, "Phouka, Phouka!" Let me see who you really are, and I'll warm you up with my large coat. Then a young bull came charging at him, thrashing his tail furiously, but Phadrig flung the coat over him, and in an instant he was peaceful as a lamb, and Phadrig instructed the kid to come to the mill that night when the moon was up, and he would have good luck.

Then Phadrig rushed there, but all he found were sacks of corn strewn across the ground; the guys had passed out and nothing had been accomplished. This continued for three consecutive nights, at which point Phadrig made up his mind to stay up and maintain watch. Later, exhausted, he laid down and slept; when he awoke in the wee hours of the morning, he found all the meal ground, even though the guys had not done so.

There was an old box in the mill, so he snuck inside it, turned the key, and peered out to see what would happen. Around twelve o'clock, six boys walked in, each with a sack of maize on his back; and after them came an old man in ragged rags, and he bade them turn the mill, and they turned until all was ground.

The next night, Phadrig told his father; the miller decided to watch with his son, and they witnessed the same occurrence.

The farmer remarked, "Now I see it is the Phouka's work, and let him labor if it pleases him, for the men are idle and lethargic and simply sleep. Tomorrow I'll take everything with me and let this terrific old Phouka take care of grinding the grain.

Now that he didn't have to pay any of his workers, the farmer's wealth skyrocketed, and he was able to grind all of his grain for free. There was tremendous interest among the locals about his wealth, but he kept quiet about the Phouka so as not to ruin his good fortune.

So Phadrig frequently visited the mill and hid in the box to observe the fairies at work; nevertheless, he felt sorry for the old Phouka in his ragged clothes, who still directed everything and had a tough time of it at times keeping the tiny Phoukas in order. The old Phouka always stood on the mill floor to give his orders to the tiny men, so Phadrig, out of love and thanks, purchased a nice suit of fabric and silk and set it there one night. He then crept into the chest to watch.

The Phouka looked at the garments and exclaimed, "How is this?" Are these meant for me?" I'm going to get made into a real gentleman.

After donning them, he walked around the house admiring his reflection. But then, all of a sudden, he recalled the corn and proceeded to grind like normal, only to stop and cry out—

"No, no. I am now officially jobless. Corn is not a task for refined gentlemen. I plan on getting out of the house to explore the world and flaunt my wardrobe. He then discarded the rags by kicking them into a corner and exited.

There was no grinding of maize that night, or the next, or the next; the little Phoukas had all fled, and the mill had gone silent. Phadrig eventually mourned the death of his longtime companion and could often be heard pleading in the fields: "Phouka, Phouka! Come back to me. Give me a look at your face. But old Phouka never returned, and Phadrig never saw his friend's face again in all the years of his life. But the farmer had made so much money that he didn't need any more help, so he sold the mill and brought up his son Phadrig to be an outstanding student and a gentleman who lived in a mansion and had his own staff. He eventually wed a stunning beauty who was rumored to be the daughter of the fairy king.

At the traditional toast to the bride's health, Phadrig noticed an unusual sight: a golden cup full of wine, sitting near him. Phadrig assumed the cup was a gift from the Phouka, and he and his bride drank the wine without hesitation after taking a peek inside. And they lived happily and prosperously ever after, guarding the golden cup as a family heirloom; it is still owned by Phadrig's descendants today.

THE CHILD OF FAIRIES

An elderly Innis-Sark resident recalled a young woman she knew who had been married for five years but had no children. And her spouse was a harsh, unpleasant man who frequently beat and mocked her since she was childless. In due time, however, she gave birth to a male child who was as stunningly handsome as an angel. And the father was so overjoyed by the arrival of his baby that he rarely left the house, opting instead to stay at home and help his wife with the household chores.

But when he rocked the cradle one day, the baby looked up at him, and, lo and behold, a big beard had grown on his face. The patriarch then yelled at his wife:

This is a demon, not a child!" You've put a bad spell on him, so stop.

And he hit her harder than he had ever hit anyone before, making her beg for help. As the thunder roared overhead, the lights went out, and two mysterious women, wearing red caps and carrying thick sticks, burst through the open door. And one of them grabbed the victim by the arms as the other beat him nearly to death.

They declared, "We are the avengers; gaze upon us and tremble; for if you ever beat your wife again, we will come and murder you." Drop on your knees and beg her forgiveness.

Then, when the terrified wretch did so, they all vanished.

Once they left, the man said, "Now, this house is no proper place for me." I'm never coming back to it.

So he left and stopped bothering his poor wife.

And then the infant in the cradle sat up straight.

Once the man leaves, he turns to his mother and says, "Now, mother. A holy well you have never seen is located nearby; you may identify it by the dense growth of green rushes covering its opening. If you go to that location, kneel down, and scream out loudly three times, an old woman will appear, and she will grant your every wish. If you do tell someone about the well and the woman, bad things will happen.

To keep her word, the mom walked to the well and yelled for help three times. Then an old lady approached and said:

"Why are you calling me, woman?"

And the frightened mother replied tremblingly—

The little one sent me, so please be good to me.

The woman invited him to join her in the well, saying, "Come down with me into the well and have no fear."

The mother extended her hand, and the other woman led her down a set of stone stairs; when they reached a large, locked door, the older woman pushed it open and commanded her to go inside. But, the mother cried out of fear.

The second voice said, "Enter and fear nothing. This is the entrance to the king's palace, and inside you will find the fairy queen, whose child you are caring for by nursing him; the king, who is also the fairy queen's husband, sits on a golden throne beside them. And don't be afraid; just don't question anything and do what you're told.

The door opened to reveal a stunning hall with a marble floor and solid gold walls, bathed in a brilliant light that made it difficult to focus the eyes. They entered another chamber, and there, at the far end, on a golden throne, was the fairy king. He was strikingly gorgeous, and his silver-clad queen was a sight to behold as she sat at his side.

This lady, is the woman who cares for your baby prince, she continued.

The monarch greeted the nurse with a warm grin, then gestured for her to take a seat before asking how she had heard of the palace.

"My son, it is who told her," the king answered angrily.

But, the monarch calmed him down and turned to one of her ladies, saying,

"Bring the other kid in here."

The woman then entered carrying an infant and deposited the child into his mother's arms.

The queen answered, "Take him; he is your own child, that we carried away because he was so beautiful, and the son you have at home is mine, a little elfish imp. You may return home with your own beautiful child in peace, knowing that he has the permanent blessing of the fairies, but I still want him back and have dispatched a man to fetch him here. The man who assaulted you was actually a messenger sent by us to effect a kid exchange. Now return home, where you will find your own true husband waiting for you with open arms, day and night.

The mother was terrified as the door opened and the man who had battered her entered. As she expressed panic, the man smiled and ordered her to calm down, eat what was provided, and leave without incident.

They took her into another room and set the table for her with golden cutlery, crystal wine goblets, and stunning blooms.

They urged us to partake in the feast that they had prepared. We can't eat it because it's been salted, and we can't eat salt.

So she ate, and she drank the red wine, and never in her life had so many beautiful and delicious things been placed before her. After the meal, she rose and folded her hands in a gesture of thanks to God, as was her custom. They managed to halt her progress and slow her down.

They screamed, "Shh! That name is off limits!"

The hallway was filled with agitated muttering. The unfortunate mother was so fascinated by the music and singing that she collapsed to the ground, looking as though she had just died. It was noontime when she regained consciousness, and she found herself standing outside her front door. And her husband came out, and led her inside by the hand. And there was her child, radiant as ever, a young prince in the making.

The spouse finally broke the silence, "Where have you been all this while?"

She responded, "It has only been an hour since I left to find my kid, whom the fairies abducted."

The man exclaimed, "One hour!" after learning that his wife and child had been missing for three years. After you left, a little, sickly creature about the size of a mushroom was placed in the cradle, and I immediately recognized it as a fairy changeling. But one day, a tailor happened to be passing by and decided to rest; and when he looked closely at the kid, the hideous malformed thing sat up fairly straight in the cradle and cried out—

It's like, 'Hey, what are you staring at? Just give me four straws, okay?

The tailor then handed him the straws. The chairs and

tables in the room started dancing as soon as the baby got his hands on them, and when he was finally exhausted, he went back to sleep in his cradle.

The tailor then continued, "Well, that child is not right; but I'll tell you what to do. Start by building a large fire.

To that end, we fabricated a fire. The tailor then locked the door, removed the poor infant from its cradle, and set it on the fireplace. As soon as the flames touched it, it screamed loudly and escaped up the chimney. I knew you'd come back to me with our own wonderful boy once everything it owned was destroyed in a fire. Now let us call upon God by name and bless our home with the sign of the Cross so that we may be spared from any further misfortune.

From that day on, the man and his wife enjoyed a life of bliss, and their son grew up to be healthy, wealthy, and successful—just as the fairy queen had promised—because the fairy blessings were bestowed upon him.

THE FAIRIES AS FALLEN ANGELS.

The islanders, like the rest of the Irish, believe that fairies are fallen angels cast out of heaven by the Lord God for their sinful hubris. And some fell into the sea, some on dry land, and some into the depths of hell, where the devil grants them knowledge and power and then dispatches them to the earth to do much evil. However, the fairies of the earth and sea are typically gentle and beautiful beings who will cause no harm if they are left alone and permitted to dance on their fairy raths in the moonlight to their own sweet music. Fire and Holy Water are revered as sacred and potent; they are the greatest protection against all things evil and a reliable test in cases of suspected witchcraft. People generally view fire as the greatest protection against witchcraft, as the demon has no power in the light. Therefore, they place a live coal beneath the churn and waft a lighted strand of straw above the cow's head if the animal appears ill. People believe that the devil no longer has influence over pigs, so they do not bother with them. When they light a candle, they make the sign of the cross because evil spirits flee the house in dread of the light.

THE FAIRY CHANGELING

A man returning home late one night noticed two women chatting in front of a house window.

One woman said, "I have left the dead child in the

cradle as you asked me, and behold, here is the second kid, take it and let me go;" A baby, wrapped in white, was laid on a sheet near the window and appeared to be sleeping secretly.

One of them said, "Wait till you have eaten some meal, and then take it to the fairy queen, as I promised, in exchange for the dead kid that we have left in the cradle beside the nurse. Wait till the moon comes up, and I'll give you the money I promised.

They walked away from the glass together. The man finally realized that there was dark sorcery at work. He silently approached the open window as soon as the women turned away, reached in, and grabbed the sleeping baby. Then, he sped home to give the baby to his mother before the women could discover what had happened. The mother's initial reaction was anger, but when he told her the story, she calmed down and placed the baby to sleep. The newborn was a healthy, gorgeous boy with a face like an angel.

The following morning, the town was in an uproar over the mysterious death of the firstborn son of the local lord. The boy had been perfectly healthy up until the night before his untimely passing. There he was, lifeless in his cradle, shrunken and wizened like a small old man, with no beauty left over when they looked at him in the morning. As a result, there was widespread mourning throughout the country, and everyone went to the funeral. The young man who had stolen the baby was among them, and he grinned when he saw the cradle with the frail infant within. The humor had finally gotten to his parents, who threatened to expel him.

On the other hand, he remarked, "Wait, put down a good fire," so they did.

Then, in front of everyone, he stepped over to the cradle and shouted loudly, "To the terrible little creature—"

"I know perfectly well who you are and where you came from; if you don't get up and leave this location right this second, I will roast you on the fire."

The kid instantly sat up and grinned at him, then ran for the exit, but the guy grabbed it and flung it in the fireplace. As soon as it was exposed to the fire, it transformed into a black kitty and disappeared up the chimney.

The man then contacted his mother to bring the second child, who turned out to be the legitimate heir and the Lord's own son. All went well when he was rescued from the fairies, and the youngster grew up to become a great lord who, in his turn, ruled the estate well. His descendants are still around today.

FAIRY WILES

When fairies abduct a pretty human kid, they usually replace them with something uglier and older looking. And as they mature, these fairy changelings become evil and greedy. In this way, unhappy parents put their child to the "fire test," expecting to see it transformed into a sod of grass if they place it in the center of the cabin and build a fire around it. If the child makes it through, however, it will be treated like a member of the family, albeit an unwelcome one; and the entire neighborhood will likely hate it because of its mischievous tendencies. The offspring of a Sidhe father and a mortal mother, on the other hand, are invariably talented and beautiful artists. Nonetheless, they are fervent and stubborn and prone to bouts of bizarre moodiness in which they crave isolation and appear to hold conversations with unseen spiritual beings.

Fairies frequently abduct beautiful young ladies from the countryside to raise their offspring. Yet, after nightfall has arrived, the mom is free to return to her own baby. She will return to her normal form after her husband throws holy water over her in the name of God as soon as she enters the house. For she sometimes hisses like a serpent, then appears dark and cloaked like one from the dead, and finally in her original shape when she takes her old seat by the hearth and nurses her infant; and the husband must not inquire, but give her food in quiet. If she is able to sleep peacefully through the third night, the fairies will no longer have any control over her, as her husband will have immediately tied a scarlet thread over the entrance to prevent them from entering and carrying her away.

THE RACE OF SIDHE.

The Sidhe dwell in the Sifra, or fairy palace of gold and crystal, in the heart of the hill, and they have been granted youth, beauty, joy, and the power over music, but they are often sad; for they remember that they were once angels in heaven but have been cast down to earth, and though they have power over all the mysteries of Nature, they must die without hope of returning to heaven, whereas mortals are assured of immortality. As a result, this one sorrow darkens their lives: a mournful envy of humanity, for while man is created immortal, the gorgeous fairy race is destined for extinction.

A great fairy chief once asked Columb-Kille if the Sidhe had any remaining prospect of regaining heaven and being reinstated to their ancient place among the angels. But the saint replied that there was no hope; their fate was predetermined, and on the day of judgment, they would pass through death into annihilation, as God's justice had decreed.

Hearing this, the fairy chief fell into a deep depression, and he and his entire court sailed away from Ireland and returned to their native Armenia to await the coming of the dreadful day of judgment, which is destined to bring the fairy race certain death on earth and no chance of regaining heaven.

Ancient Sidhe superstitions hold the western region of Ireland to be especially holy. People adore the beautiful glens, the towering mountains rising from the sea, the islands sanctified by the memory of a saint, and the green hills on which Finvarra holds court. Every lake and mountain has its legend of the spirit-land, some holy traditions of a saint, or some historical memory of a national hero who flourished in the great old days when Ireland had native chiefs and native swords to protect her; and amongst the Western Irish, in particular, the old superstitions of their ancestors are revered with a reverence that is almost religious. Finvarra, the fairy king, is still believed to reign over all the Western fairies, while Onagh is the fairy queen. Her golden hair brushes the ground, and she wears a robe of silver gossamer that sparkles as if covered in diamonds, but is actually covered in dew drops.

The queen is more beautiful than any woman on Earth, but Finvarra prefers mortal women. He lures them to his fairy palace with the subtle allure of fairy music, for no one can resist its power, and they are destined to belong to the fairies for all eternity. Their acquaintances lament for them as if they were deceased, but in reality they are living happily in the fairy palace with silver columns and crystal walls at the base of the hill.

The young men who have heard the fairy harp become possessed by a spirit of music that follows them to their deaths and grants them strange power over the souls of men. This was the case with the celebrated poet Carolan. He acquired the entire magical melody of his notes by spending the night on a fairy rath, where he dreamed of fairy music, and by playing the airs from memory upon awakening. Thus, he had the ability to drive men mad with laughter or to make them weep as if for the deceased, and no one before or since has played the enchanting fairy music like Carolan, the sweet Irish musician.

Another man heard the fairy music while sleeping on a rath, and he was haunted by the melody day and night until he went insane and lost all interest in life because he yearned to be with the fairies again so he could hear them sing. So, one day, driven to despair by the insanity of desire, he hurled himself from the cliff into the mountain lake near the fairy rath, where he perished and was never seen again.

In the Western Islands, it is believed that the enchantment of fairy music is so potent that anyone who hears it is compelled to follow it, and the young girls are enticed by the music to dance all night with

Finvarra, the king, though they are found fast asleep in bed the next morning, yet with a vivid memory of everything they had seen and heard; and some say that, while with the fairies, the young women learn the strange secrets of love potions, by which they can cast

It is a lovely notion that the Irish airs, which are so plaintive, mournful, and tear-inducing, are merely the recollected echoes of the spirit music that had the power to lure souls to the fairy mansions and hold them captive with the sweet enchantment of the melody.

QUEEN MAEVE

The Bardic Legends provide a remarkable account of a figure that appeared to Maeve, queen of Connaught, on the eve of battle.

A tall, attractive woman suddenly appeared before the queen's chariot. She wore a green robe fastened with a golden bodkin, had a golden fillet on her head, and held seven brilliant gold braids for the Dead. Her skin was as white as the snow that descends at night; her teeth were as pearls; her lips were as red as the berries of the mountain ash; her golden hair fell to the ground; and her voice was as sweet as a golden harp string played by a deft hand.

"Who are you, woman?" questioned the monarch in shock.

Abbey Theatre Emblem, 1904. /Nwoodcut By Elinor Mary Monsell, Commissioned By W.B. Yeats For The Abbey Theatre, 1904. It Depicts Queen Maeve Hunting

She responded, "I am Feithlinn, the fairy prophetess of the Rath of Cruachan."

"It is well, O prophetess Feithlinn," Maeve said, "but what do you foresee concerning our hosts?"

The prophetess responded, "I foresee violence, I foresee power, and I foresee defeat."

The queen exclaimed, "My messengers have brought me excellent news; my army is strong and my warriors are well-trained." However, declaring the truth, O prophetess, for my soul is fearless."

The second time, the prophetess replied, "I foresee

bloodshed; I foresee triumph!"

"But I have nothing to fear from the Ultonians," said the queen. "My messengers have arrived, and my foes are terrified." Yet, declare the truth, O prophetess, so that our hosts may comprehend it."

The prophetess responded for the third time, "I anticipate carnage, conquest, and death!"

Indignantly, the queen replied, "Then it does not pertain to me, your malevolent prophecy."

"Be it thine, and bear the consequences."

As she spoke, the clairvoyant maiden vanished, and the queen no longer saw her.

Queen Maeve was cruelly murdered by her own kinsman at Lough Rea by the Shannon in retaliation for the military aid she had rendered to the king of Ulster; there is an island in the lake where the spot where the great queen was murdered is marked, and which is still referred to by the locals as—the stone of the dead queen.

Maeve, the great monarch of Connaught, occupies a prominent position in Bardic Legends. When she went into battle, it is said that she rode in an open car accompanied by four chariots—one in front, one behind, and one on each side—so that the golden assion on her head and her royal robes would not be soiled by the dust of the horse's hooves or the foam of the fiery steeds; for all the sovereigns of Ireland wore a diadem in battle, as well as in the festal and public assemblies.

THE FAIRY DOCTOR

If an otherwise healthy child abruptly droops and shrivels, a fairy doctor must be summoned immediately. Young women who experience a rapid decline are also said to be "fairy-struck," as they are desired in Fairy-Land as brides for a chief or prince, causing them to pine away without apparent cause until death.

In addition to the Wind, the Evil Eye and the Evil Wind are lethal influences. The malevolent power of the Wind is known as a fairy-blast, whereas a victim of the Evil Eye is said to have been "overlooked."

The fairy doctor must determine which of these three conditions the patient is experiencing. The fairy-stroke, the fairy-blast, or the Evil Eye; however, he may not accept payment for his opinion. In exchange for assistance rendered, he is compensated with gifts of gratitude.

A person who sought the advice of a renowned fairy doctor describes the healing process as follows during the interview:

"The doctor always seems to be anticipating and fully aware of your arrival. He requests that you take a seat, and after staring intently at your face for a few moments, he begins his presentation. He selects three three-inch-long rods of witch hazel and labels them "For the Stroke," "For the Wind," and "For the Evil Eye." This is done to determine which of these three ills you suffer from. He then removes his coat, shoes, and hosiery, rolls up his shirt sleeves, and prays earnestly while facing the sun. After prayer, he takes a dish of purified water and places it by the fire, then kneeling, he places the three marked hazel rods into the fire and leaves them there until they are completely consumed by the flames. Incessantly, he prays, and when the sticks are extinguished, he rises and confronts the sun in silent prayer with his eyes raised and his hands crossed. With the end of one of the burned rods, he then draws a circle on the floor, within which he stands with a dish of pure water. Into this, he throws the three hazel rods while intently observing the outcome. As soon as one descends, he prays to the sun and, removing the rod from the water, declares the cause of the patient's illness. Then, he grinds the rod into powder, places it in a bottle filled with water from the dish, and utters an incantation or invocation over it with his hands clasped over the bottle in a low voice. No one, however, knows what the words of the invocation are; they are kept as sacred mysteries and have been passed down from father to son for countless generations, since antiquity. The elixir is then given to be conveyed home and consumed at midnight that same night in solitude and silence. The bottle must never contact the ground, and the person carrying it must remain silent and never turn around until they reach their home. The remaining two rods are buried in the ground in an unidentified location. He treats the patient with herbs if none of the three sticks penetrate. Vervain, eyebright, and yarrow are popular remedies, and the adept is aware of their potent properties; however, the words and petitions he utters over them are kept secret, and only he knows whether they are good or evil, addressed to a deity or a demon."

These are the visible mysteries exhibited by the fairy healer as he casts his spells and charms. Other fairy doctors, however, only conduct the mysteries in private and do not permit anyone to witness their method of operation or the act of prayer.

If a potion is made from botanicals, it must be purchased with silver, whereas charms and incantations are never purchased, or they would lose their potency. However, a gift may be acknowledged as an expression of gratitude.

THE FAIRY SPY

Occasionally, fairies disguise themselves as elderly men and women to obtain access to homes, where they can observe and snoop, enchant the butter, kidnap the children, and abduct young women as fairy brides.

There was a man in the west who was incapacitated for seven years, unable to work and requiring assistance to move. Nonetheless, he ingested a tremendous amount of food, and as a result of widespread pity, people were constantly bringing him a variety of delicious foods, which he devoured without gaining strength.

Now, on Sundays, when the family went to church, they locked him up but left him with plenty of food, as no one was home to assist him. One Sunday, however, they left the chapel earlier than usual, and as they walked along the shore, they saw a large throng of strangers hurling, and in the midst of them, hurling and running and leaping, was the sick man, as healthy and merry as he had ever been. They called out to him, and he turned around to face them, but he vanished at that moment.

Therefore, the family hurried home, unlocked the door, and went directly to the man's room, where they found him in bed as usual, emaciated and unable to move; however, he had consumed all the food and was now pleading for more. This enraged the family, who shouted out, "You have deceived us!" You are in league with the witches, but we'll shortly see who you really are: if you don't get out of bed immediately, we'll build a fire, lay you on it, and force you to walk."

Then he cried out and roared, but he was captured and dragged to the flames. When he realized they were serious, he jumped up and ran to the door, and before they could contact him, he vanished and was never seen again.

Now that they knew he was in league with the devil, they burned his bed and all of his belongings and poured holy water over the chamber. And after everything was burned, only a black stone with peculiar markings remained. Without a doubt, he performed his spells in this manner. And because the people feared it and gave it to the cleric, who still has it to this day, there is no doubt about the story's veracity.

And the priest knows the secret meaning of the strange signs that give power to the stone, but he will not disclose it to anyone, lest the people attempt to use the stone's power and the power of the signs to cast unlawful spells.

CHARM AGAINST FAIRY STROKES

If a fairy-stroke is suspected, a very ancient and potent talisman can be employed to great effect.

Place three rows of salt on a table, each row containing three equal measures. The caster then encircles the rows of salt with his arm, leaning his head over them as he recites the Lord's Prayer three times over each row for a total of nine repetitions. Then he takes the hand of the person who has been enchanted and says, "By the power of the Father, the Son, and the Holy Spirit, let this disease depart and the evil spirits' spell be destroyed!" I adjure and command that you leave this man alone [named]. In the name of God, I pray; in the name of Christ, I implore; and in the name of God's Holy Spirit, I command and compel you to turn around and release this individual! Amen! Amen! Hallelujah!"

KEEP THE COINS SECRET

In most cases throughout Wales, blabbing only results in a loss of fairy favor. There's a story about a boy who spotted fairies under a bridge in Anglesea and benefited from their kindness. A groat (a coin worth 4 pence) would always be waiting for him on a specific stone of Cymmunod Bridge after he went to collect his father's cows from the pasture each morning. The frequent appearance of coins in the boy's possession raised suspicions with his father, who once spent the Sabbath interrogating him about the source of his wealth. Even though the youngster pursued this lead by visiting the area frequently, he never did find any money on the bridge or make amends with the angry Tylwyth Teg. His betrayal of the secret cost him their favor.

There is a similar tale about a young woman named Anne William Francis in the parish of Bassalleg, who went out at night into a little wooded area close to her home and encountered a group of fairies dancing in the grass. She brought them a bucket of water since she figured they'd appreciate it. The following time she went, she was given a shilling, and so on, for several more visits until she had twenty-one total. But when her mom found the money, she suspected theft and questioned her about it. Although she initially denied telling, the youngster eventually admitted that she had gotten the money from fairies after her mother threatened to beat her. She never received any more after that.

CONCLUSION

Through this exploration of the world of fairies, I hope you have come to embrace the magic that they bring into your lives. We have learned to appreciate the beauty of nature and the wonder it holds, as well as the gentle guidance of the fairy realm. Whether we choose to work with fairies in our rituals, connect with them through offerings and divination, or appreciate their mythical wonder, they serve as a reminder to see the world in a different light.

As we go forth, let us continue to embrace the magic of fairies and the lessons they teach us. May we always seek out the enchantment in the world around us, and may the magic of the fairy realm continue to inspire us to see things with a sense of wonder and awe.

BIBLIOGRAPHY

Morgan, Adrian, *Toads and Toadstools: The Natural History, Mythology and Cultural Oddities of This Strange Association.* Ten Speed Press. 1996

Hall, Alaric, *Elves in Anglo-Saxon England: Matters of Belief, Health, Gender and Identity.* Anglo Saxon Series. 2009.

Franklin, Anna. *The Illustrated Encyclopedia of Fairies.* Vega. 2003.

Briggs, Katherine. *A Dictionary of Fairies.* Penguin UK. 1977.

Godwin, William. *Lives of the Necromancers.* Frederick J. Mason, London. 1834.

Westrop, Thos J. *A Folklore Survey of County Clare: Fairies and Fairy Forts and Mounds.* Folklore, Vol. 21, No. 2. 1910.

Lady Wilde. *Ancient Legends Mystic Charms and Superstitions of Ireland.* Chatto and Windus, London. 1919.

Sikes, Wirt. *British Goblins: Welsh Folk-Lore, Fairy Mythology, Legends And Traditions.* Clowes & Sons. 1880.

www.ingramcontent.com/pod-product-compliance
Lightning Source LLC
Chambersburg PA
CBHW060036050426

42448CB00012B/3038